TEACHING
REFLECTIONS

Carleen Osher

Illustrations by
Pete Chadwell

Rainbow Books, Inc.

Library of Congress Cataloging in Publication

Osher, Carleen.
   Teaching reflections / Carleen Osher.
         p.   cm.
      ISBN 0-935834-80-X : $12.95
      1. Teaching—Miscellanea.   2. Teachers—Attitudes—Miscellanea.
   I. Title.
   LB1027.077   1992
   371.1'02—dc20   91-44443
                                                                         CIP

TEACHING REFLECTIONS
By Carleen Osher
© Copyright 1992 by Carleen Osher
Illustrations by Pete Chadwell
Cover Design by Therese Cabell
Interior Design by Marilyn Ratzlaff
Published by Rainbow Books, Inc.
P. O. Box 430
Highland City, FL 33846-0430

Printed in the United States of America

Recognizing the importance of preserving the written word,
Rainbow Books, Inc., by policy, prints all of its first editions
on acid-free (Neutral pH) paper.

CONTENTS

Topics Covered

BEGINNINGS AND ENDINGS

The morning bells herald the beginning of the school day while later the raucous ring breaks into your thoughts, hurries lessons through the hours and finally signals the end. The rush of it all, you know that quality moments in teaching don't fit neatly into those time cubicles but slip in the door with a shy smile, hide behind widened eyes or settle in with a spontaneous hug. The beginnings, sometimes late or unexpected, offer a rare journey; the endings are the letting go times, the growing times. Teaching is filled with the measuring of successes and the punctuating of failures. Listen to the beginnings and reflect on the endings. Both are the unseen treasures that let you smile during a day where bells pace your moments.

❦

If one advances confidently in the direction
of his dreams, and endeavors to live the life which
he has imagined, he will meet with a success
unexpected in the common hours.

Henry David Thoreau

SHADOWS

To teach well is to share the dream about what can be, not what is. The past is locked with yesterday's decisions and actions; it cannot be changed. The present is so close sometimes students feel surrounded by the immediacy and helpless in its nearness. But the future offers time for thought, and reflection; change becomes possible and within reach. Youth will experience growth with or without learning. The master teacher senses that the vision of the future is like the shadow of a tree, one does not exist without the other.

❦

I have a dream.

Martin Luther King

MASTER TEACHER

Within the word teacher you will discover the individual words "teach," "each," and "ache." Isn't that how you spend much of your time?

You have been trained to *teach*. Knowledge of learning styles, motivation, discipline techniques and learning theory are the tools you trade in. You know that fine teaching is the blending of an intangible, art with the measurables of a science. You are a highly skilled professional, not just anyone could do what you do.

Experience has taught you to focus upon each student individually. *Each* has the uniqueness of a snowflake; no two are identical. Some are cold and distant; others melt at a word or touch. You try to reach each student by offering the tantalizing gifts of knowledge, wonder and caring. Though you will find yourself drawn to some students more than others, each will walk this way but once; you deal in the precious.

As you come to understand and care for an individual child, sometimes you will *ache*. Humankind's inhumanities: abuse, poverty and cruelty squeeze your heart. You realize that, in reality, your caring may only offer a momentary haven but no cure.

Know your heartache will keep your senses alive and aware, your actions positive and meaningful and your spirit laced with compassion and gentleness. No one ever promised good teaching would be easy. And, so it is, that "teach," "each," and "ache" reside within every master teacher.

❦

If I had a child who wanted to be a teacher, I would bid him Godspeed as if he were going into war. For indeed the war against prejudice, greed and ignorance is eternal, and those who dedicate themselves to it give their lives no less because they may live to see some fraction of the battle won.

James Hilton

CREATIVITY

Creativity, the child within, demands attention. She whistles, nags at boredom and answers sassily. Days of endless dittos, intercom messages, textbook materials, departmental memos and routine are all shattered by her joyous laughter and, often, unexpected arrival. Rarely does she seek an invitation; that's too planned. In fact, sometimes she leaves right in the middle of her visit and does not have the time to pick up after herself. She can be unruly, messy, and unpredictable. She does not like to hang out with facts, statistics or anything written in columns. She loves questions, wrestles with direct answers wondering if things must be *that* way and stamps her feet sighing when someone points out a line is crooked. (She cannot think straight.) She loves laughter, energy, and play. She doesn't complete everything she starts, she hates following directions step by step and often appears lost. She likes colors, all shapes except perhaps squares and enjoys the noise of excitement. She dislikes punctuality, three-piece suits and ties that *always* match. When she knocks on the classroom door, good teachers let her in with a smile knowing she often holds the key to learning. Besides, if not invited in, she may draw bars on the windows and locks on the doors before she rushes off giggling.

❣

Creative people exhibit a continuous
discontent with uniformity.

Glenn Van Ekeren

FALL

Fall quarter always begins with such flurry. The treasures of summer have been spent restoring expended energy, refueling the supply of enthusiasm and reassessing old programs. During vacation days file by like good books, each predicating the next. Page after page turns until the final chapter arrives, giving us a twinge of disappointment but, too, a sense of completeness.

The air breathes crisper; the nights hug us cooler. It's time to return and start again. For the veteran teacher fall signals another year of melding ideals and realities with flashes of cynicism and periods of sensitivity. You know you face nine months of long hours, and much hard work seasoned liberally with humor, anger, patience, endurance, fatigue, and joy. You will survive.

For the new teacher, fall is a time of great excitement, extraordinary enthusiasm and boundless energies, the highs higher and lows almost unendurable. Some will survive. Together, old and new, we bond and greet the students.

❦

The beginning is the most important part of the work.

(English proverb)

BRIDGES

The most concerned teachers among us have learned to skillfully navigate the channels of communication by carefully listening to the constant flow of words around them. They can hear the shift in a message and read the hidden undercurrents swirling beneath the quiet surface waters. Stagnant thoughts, murky meanings and drifts in the conversation are all silently assessed.

With patience and skill born of experience, they know a good, strong span of listening bridges almost any gap of troubled water. Realizing this partnership asks nothing from them but time and concentration while promising a foothold of understanding on the other shore, these teachers hear what others do not have time for and build bridges others do not think possible.

❧

The greatest compliment that was ever paid me
was when one asked what I thought and
attended my answer.

Henry David Thoreau

GIFTS

Teachers are the lucky ones. During the day they dispense gifts of time which can change the shade of a moment, chase the clouds away from the sun or maybe, just maybe, be the best present given to that student all day.

Dignity for Robert who tries and fails
Hugs for Ann who lives with fear
Gentleness for Beth who has been handled roughly
Curiosity for Timothy who never wonders
Inspiration for Jamie who wants to quit
Self-esteem for Tony who feels worthless
Friendship for Heather who is all alone
Courage for Mark who is afraid to try
Laughter for Marty who rarely smiles
Trust for Amy who has been betrayed
Integrity for Kelly who is learning to lie
Excitement for Benjamin who shows little emotion
Peace for Trina who lives in constant battle
Recognition for Jimmy who goes unnoticed
Patience for Brenda who struggles to learn
Confidence for Peter who is always unsure
Forgiveness for Theodore who loses his temper
Pride for Jonathon who finally does well
Kindness for Meagan whom life has wounded
Compassion for Melissa who suffers in silence
Solitude for Lincoln who is never alone
Pleasure for Whitney who knows little joy

These gifts are lovingly wrapped and tied with care. As teachers we know we are only returning what was once given to us.

❦

There are only two lasting bequests we can hope to give our children. One is roots; the other is wings.

Hodding Carter

PIECES

Rarely is a fine English teacher just an English teacher or a good biology teacher just a biology teacher. Within the excellent exist many masters. There flows the creativity of the gifted artist who paints with symmetry and passion each canvas as if it were the last. There shines the love of children which recognizes the uniqueness and joyfulness of life. There giggles the comedian who allows for the whimsical and balances seriousness. There resides the judge who is known for fairness and patience in trial after trial. There practices the athlete who knows making the team is not easy. There rests the wise one who understands the difference between what seems right and what is right and is not afraid of the choice. There plays the actor who knows life is seasoned with emotion and dramatic flare. And lastly, there lives the craftsman who uses quality as a measure and takes pleasure in that which is not just done, but done well. The master teacher is never *just* a teacher.

❦

The mediocre teacher tells. The good teacher explains.
The superior teacher demonstrates.
The great teacher inspires.

William Arthur Ward

PERCEPTIONS

WHAT DO YOU DO FOR A LIVING?

Teacher 1: I am a high-priced babysitter.

Teacher 2: I am just a teacher.

Teacher 3: I am working with the world's future.

❦

Man is what he believes.

Anton Chekhov

RESERVATIONS ONLY

The bell rings, the period begins and, wonder of wonders, it's a full house. Everyone is present! Normally, with attendance being what it is, there is at least one empty seat. However, not today... thirty plus. Some students impatiently show their reservations and disdain while others courteously sit with a disguised hunger for knowledge; they wait for you to whet their appetites with the teaser before you begin serving up the main course. (Inwardly, you are well aware that a few of your patrons will select only what they want from today's menu no matter how well you have prepared the full entré and no matter how carefully you have explained that there is no such thing as a la carte in your establishment.) You quietly recognize those customers who demand not only impeccable service but individual attention.

Then, just as you start stirring the broth, the door swings open and in walks a new student. Greeting her with a smile, (while privately noting to refresh the counselor's mind about your class loads) you explain to her that, at the moment, you have no extra seating. Until there is an opening, she will have to sit at the back table. Efficiently, clearing the stack of books and papers which you were sorting earlier, you motion her to take her seat. Then you begin . . . again. Welcome to El Restaurante de Educación, where all are seated and served.

❦

I want every laborer in my realm to be able
to put a fowl in the pot on Sunday.

Henry IV

"SOULAR" POWER

Teaching without the joy of laughter is like a long, restless night without sleep. Weariness, impatience and surface anger constantly interrupt the hours. Time plods by, work stacks up while the energy required to "get through it" evaporates. Then, the absurd: forcing yourself to focus and concentrate, you take the first essay off a large stack and begin to read, "Of all my teachers I admire Mrs. Blake, my chemistry teacher, the most because she has to spend hours in stinky lavatories (sic) with all kinds of icky smells, and she doesn't seem to mind!" (And your colleague Blake does not even know that some regard her job as latrine duty! You can't wait to tease her.) A smile threatens your face and nuzzles your heart; within that moment you feel a bit better, less tired and happier. In each teaching day seek the joy of genuine laughter. "Soular" power will help restore your energy, perspective and purpose.

❦

Laughter is a tranquilizer with no side effects.

Arnold Glasow

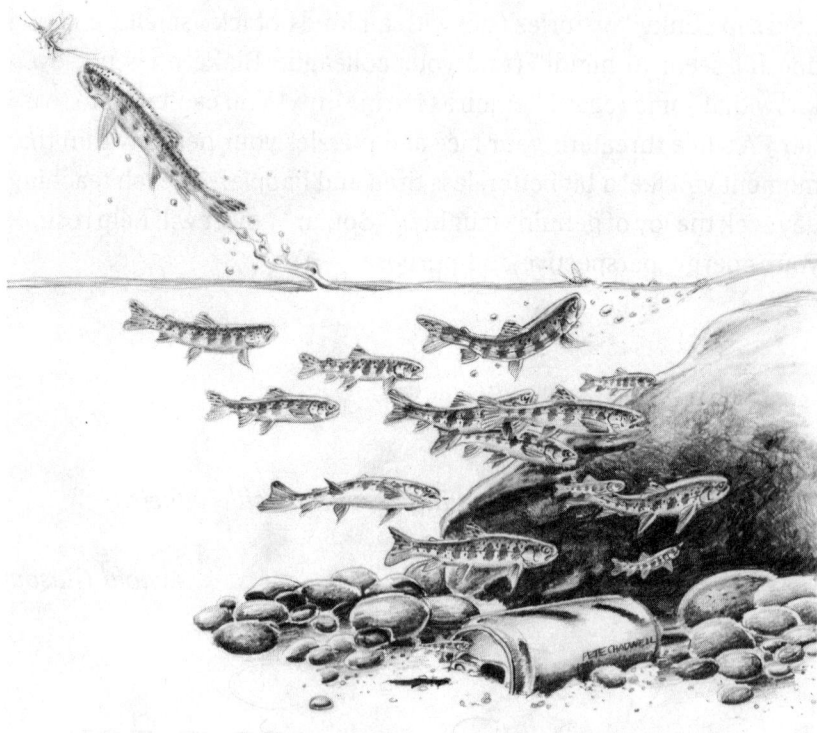

NETWORKS

Every school harbors a few master teachers, but have you ever noticed how some faculties anchor themselves with more liveliness, excellence and caring? These staffs sift through the unimportant bringing to the surface the meaning of education. Consider how the line of a net is intertwined; though each length is bound by ties, space surrounds it. Good faculties know a single line cast out may lure a solitary catch, but a net will gather many. Like the weave of a net, not every staff member is in contact with every other, but each is tied to a few colleagues. Each teacher allows space for growth and flexibility but recognizes the strength of the weave.

Likewise, students schooled by the netting of a faculty find slipping by more difficult. Most are held and touched by the webbing but can see from within the safety of net the "outside" world and its challenges and promises. Just as easily as the net has been cast out, so may the master staff overturn it, releasing the students to the open waters that beckon. Good faculties know that the net works.

❦

We must have . . . a place where children can have
a whole group of adults they can trust.

Margaret Mead

LINKS

Beautifully constructed, intricate works of art . . . formidable barriers threatening trespassers . . . rough hewn, serviceable entries to areas not openly accessible . . . gates are the lock, latch or link. They can be the best of protectors, the cruelest of prison guards or the beckoning bridge to friendliness. Opened quietly, slammed shut unexpectedly or climbed over expertly, gates are as strong as the owner and as necessary as privacy.

The caring, sensitive teacher has learned to be the best of gatekeepers. She is one who can find keys to locks rusted shut from lack of care or can carefully close gates blown open on windy days. This master gatekeeper knows the keys are often found in the heart, understands that maintenance is located on the shelf next to personal respect and that freedom is found in sharing the opening and shutting of passages.

❧

No one can develop freely in this world and find a full life without feeling understood by at least one person.

Dr. Paul Tournier

HOLIDAYS

The Monday after the Thanksgiving holiday rudely shakes you awake. You must squeeze much teaching and learning, framed by infinite patience, into the next three busy weeks. The Christmas countdown compacts your days; restlessness lingers in the hallways and lurks in the classrooms. As the vacation draws nearer, your skills and sanity may be challenged. Like the packages under the tree, surprises lie in wait. Fun sparkles in students' eyes while lessons compete with what's in each present and who's coming to visit. When the last bell on the final day rings, sighs and laughter surround you. It's hard to explain how holidays always arrive just at the right moment.

❦

But I heard him exclaim, as he drove out of sight,
"Happy Christmas to all and to all a good night!"

Clement C. Moore

TEACHING REFLECTIONS ❦ 27

❦ TEACHING REFLECTIONS

THE GUEST

Wisdom does not just happen and is not a gift given at birth. Though having no shape or size, she is highly selective and does not come to everyone. Wisdom is a guest only to those who think, who listen, who question, who seek the truth. She delights in those who make mistakes and try again, who take risks and share the bounty, who value integrity and cannot be bought, and who love inspite of and because of. She is the bandage of pain and the center of joy. Although she does not mind being shared, her visits are often short, for she does not like gossip, impatience or meanness as roommates. She prefers quiet to brashness and balance to extremes. The veteran teacher knows wisdom is the best of friends and the worst of enemies; she is the shadow of experience. And when the sun is brightest, she offers us respite from the heat.

❦

Knowledge comes, but wisdom lingers.

Tennyson

ATTITUDES

Because schools are microcosms of society, teachers can end up in buildings or districts where they experience fear rather than growth, insecurity rather than security, and stagnation rather than innovation. Systems can be liberating or oppressing, forgiving or vindictive. One faculty may have a sense of aliveness while another is unmoved by vision. Schools reflect the nations of the terrorist, the revolutionist, the conservative and the liberal. For one individual to single-handedly change a nation is as rare as it is for one teacher to change a building or district. But just as the revolutionist in the oppressive nation, change must start somewhere. One step or word is better than none. Teacher, diplomat, soldier, prisoner of war, actions and attitudes make a difference.

❦

The great end of life is not knowledge but action.

Thomas Henry Huxley

EVER EXPERIENCED

1. .... Confusing a student's identity during a parent conference?
2. .... A one-hundred-and-four paper fever?
3. .... The perfect lesson plan that becomes a natural disaster?
4. .... Taking a spitwad and jamming it back into the shooter's mouth?
5. .... Laughing and enjoying your students so much you don't get to the day's lesson?
6. .... Putting so much time into your teaching "it" becomes your personal life?
7. .... Bombing during your evaluation observation?
8. .... Returning the same verbal abuse you just encountered?
9. .... Showing a film so you could grade papers?
10. .... Teaching with authority a factual error within your content area?
11. .... Acting some days more like the resident gestapo than a teacher?
12. .... Wishing for "overs" in a certain situation?
13. .... Feeling relief when you find out a certain student is absent?
14. .... Telling someone what you do for a living and then accepting his sympathy?
15. .... Taking a mental health day just because you are too tired to deal with "it"?
16. .... Avoiding enforcing a school rule because you don't want to be involved in another confrontation?
17. .... Thinking up an excuse so you don't have to attend another meeting?
18. .... Sneaking "extra" copies from the copy machine?
19. .... Misplacing the dittos you just ran off and really need?

❦

We find it hard to believe that other people's thoughts are as silly as our own, but they probably are.

John Kenneth Galbraith

EDUCATION

To be able to be caught up into the world of thought —
that is education.

Edith Hamilton

A child miseducated is a child lost.

John Kennedy

Why should society feel responsible only for the education of
children, and not for the education of all adults of every age?

Erich Fromm

Education is a social process . . . education is growth . . .
Education is not preparation for life; education is life itself.

John Dewey

The secret of education is respecting the pupil.

Waldo Emerson

The aim of education should be to teach us rather how to think than
what to think, — rather to improve minds, so as to enable us to think for
ourselves, than to load the memory with the thoughts of other men.

James Beattie

The business of education is not to make the young perfect in any one of the sciences, but to open and dispose their minds as may best make them capable of any, when they shall apply themselves.

John Locke

Excellence in education is not so much teaching a child what to think, but how to think, so that he goes on seeking, choosing, and thinking, so developing the persistent habit of inquiry and reasoning, and if, years later, the knowledge he has acquired in school has become irrelevant to his purpose, dated, or forgotten, he still has the ability to acquire new knowledge, to understand events more clearly and to adapt himself to new circumstances. Quality education is not just providing information, it is developing wiser minds.

E. J. Oliver

TANDEMS

Agility, endurance, balance, awareness of road conditions, knowledge of signals and teamwork produce the veteran tandem rider with the most skill and fewest tumbles and scratches. Sometimes you will find yourself peddling as fast as possible with the person behind you pushing for even greater speeds. Though your legs tire, exhileration fuses your energies. At other times, you feel that you are peddling alone, pulling your uncooperative partner along just for the ride. Then the seats are switched and someone else is in the front, and you are in for a ride, bumpy or smooth. Riding the tandem, like teaching, improves with experience.

Remember, the advantage of being a tandem rider is not only the sharing of the responsibility and joys of the journey, but if one falls off, there is someone else there to help him get up.

❧

Friendship is a sheltering tree.

Samuel Taylor Coleridge

LONG TREK

After the Christmas holidays fewer surprises await you; most packages have been unwrapped and their contents revealed. Like the winter sleep, the halls are quieter, the learning more intense, and the interruptions fewer. The excitement that embraced the first school day and the season's first snowfall are memories. Breathe deeply of the chilled air, enjoy the calmness and pace your energies, for the long trek has begun.

❦

Great works are performed not by strength,
but by perseverance.

Samuel Johnson

REST

Sometimes the weight created by the stress of teaching is enormous. Think about the word "stress." Drop some of the excess baggage you are carrying . . . S T R E $\cancel{S}$ $\cancel{S}$. Rearrange your priorities S T R E and get some . . . R E S T!

(numbers above STRE: 3 4 1 2)

❦

Less is more.

Robert Browning

SECRETS

Statistics indicate that the average teacher in the United States is in his or her forties. Our ranks are growing older; many of us have taught fifteen or twenty years and recognize the routine, predictable and cyclical nature of education. An inner voice may whisper, "Is this all there is? Will I still be doing this in ten or fifteen years from now?"

Time and opportunity no longer seem to be on an endless horizon. We struggle with the uncertainty of our future and the unexpected restlessness of our spirit. What was a central force in earlier years, may not hold the same magnetism it once did; a feeling of job disillusionment echoes from within.

Teacher education does not just happen in the method classes or on the college campuses; be your own teacher. Take time to reassess and reprioritize your goals. If teaching is no longer the center it once was, that is okay. It is time to not only be good at what you do, but who you are. Explore what makes you happy. Take a risk, grow, laugh, and love. You will pass this way but once.

❦

The deepest personal defeat suffered by human beings is constituted by the difference between what one was capable of becoming and what one has become.

Ashley Montagu

ON THE FRONT

The cold, grey dawn, promising only another day on the front, seeps across the horizon. Silent alarms signal the first sign of light.

Quietly many of our rank and file begin their day by planning a successful foray into off-limits territory. They wear the camouflage clothing of the professional, crisp, clean and conservative. (No one will be able to accuse them of wrongdoing because no one will catch them doing wrong.)

Their target? Achieving undetected entry to the state of the art technology which is housed and relentlessly guarded in the inner sanctums of the administrative offices. To underscore that such a transgression will not be tolerated, the building authorities have guaranteed retribution for any trespassers noting that the penalty promises swiftness and severity. The exact punishment of such a breech is unknown, but the phrase "execution at dawn" whispers through the grapevine. Consequently, great care is taken by these dedicated, intrepid colleagues who risk so much.

Access is gained by the stealth of an early arrival, the aplomb of a nonchalant greeting, the confidence of the businesslike demeanor, and the skill of the quick fake around the corner. If all goes well, another high tech theft will come off without a hitch; perpetrator undetected and mission accomplished: thirty, easily read photocopies of the day's assignment. And so it is, another skirmish in the Great Copy Machine Wars ends with professionalism intact and copies secreted into the classroom.

❧

War is hell.

William Tecumseh Sherman

POLITICS

Strangely, we reside in a political arena. The controlling body, the school board, is elected. Some parents are more powerful than others, some teachers more influential than their colleagues. Administrators, by the very nature of their jobs, must be politically aware. You may find yourself making a classroom, curriculum or instructional decision for political reasons rather than educational ones. Introspectively, a vague dissatisfaction may settle beside you like an unwanted shadow you cannot shrug off. However, the reality is some issues are not winnable and may not be worth your fight. There will be times when the strength of your integrity will prompt you to speak out and be heard. Your spirit will soar. Other times your voice will be ignored or your actions countered; the sting of political reprisal may wound you. At times you will choose to stand idly by while your colleagues run the gauntlet without you.

Being in a political arena is not easy for teachers. Learn to pick and choose your battles carefully. You cannot be on every front; your time and energies are limited. Allow yourself the freedom not to fight every battle, but do not give in to total surrender.

❦

We hear of a silent generation, more concerned with
security than integrity, with conforming than performing,
with limiting than creating.

Thomas J. Watson

PETE
CHADWELL
1989

MOUNTAINS

Often the evenings before a mountain trek are spent in anticipation of the journey. Plans are made, routes retraced and supplies checked and rechecked. The hours of preparation give way to tiredness. When sleep finally comes, visions of the terrain with reflections of the difficult junctures crowd the night's peace. The climber, like the teacher, must enjoy the journey as much as the destination. Breathe deeply of the morning air, be planned for the climb, but allow for the unexpected.

❦

It's a bad plan that can't be changed.

Publilius Syrus

PATIENCE

During the school week greet each day by drinking deeply from the well of patience. On the good days this act is unnecessary; on the bad days sometimes your last ounce of patience has been swallowed, and you return to find a dry well. The side effects — temper, frustration and sarcasm — surge into the void and angrily lap the edges spilling over into the classroom. Reality will tell you that no individual is granted a daily quota of patience, but teaching sorely tests that idea. Why is it a teacher can run out of something that has no measure?

❦

Patience is power. With time and patience the
mulberry leaf becomes silk.

Chinese Proverb

LEARNIN'

Learning, like good teaching, does not always come easily. Sometimes it is downright painful, and sometimes, it does not come at all. We are told by some learning is the beginning; yet, others loudly proclaim it as the end result. As teachers, we may not know whether we are on the starting line or the finish line. We spend innumerable hours weighing and defining learning to prove to others (and sometimes ourselves) that it exists. Obviously, we can't be paid for the immeasurables, so we "libitimize" learning (dissect the whole into little, itty, bitty pieces). Hence, the powerful testing procedures: S.A.T., A.C.T. The list is enormous and the test results not only herald our "successes and failures" but claim to predict the possible future success of each student.

In theory some seem to believe if they can measure each grain of sand then they can take credit for the whole beach rather than a desert. Yet, in the recesses of our minds lingers doubt. Though Trivial Pursuit is a national pastime, can it be a learning barometer, too? Could it be that in our attempt to validate and measure our results, we have overlooked the significant? Isn't the difference between a desert and a beach not the minute grains of sand, but the water lapping the shores?

❦

Nature has buried truth at the bottom of the sea.

Democritus, attributed

ANGER

Anger never arrives alone. She has a lot of friends with whom she travels. Besides, her arrival is always someone else's fault. She hits, pinches, glares, smirks, talks back and sulks if things don't go her way. Her gang includes the hitmen called Revenge, Get Even and You'll Be Sorry. Though she has no age, she comes in every size and shape. She is a thief taking what she wants when she wants. She ignores good manners and has little sense of time and place. When she enters the room, even if she is quiet, you can feel her. She acts most unhappy when she goes unnoticed.

Teachers are no stranger to Anger. She sometimes comes with the territory. However, though the veteran teacher realizes that Anger should be let out on occasion, they watch her carefully knowing she can steal patience, pride and time often replacing them with pain, hurt and fear. The master teacher understands swallowing angry words is often easier than having to eat them.

❦

It is better to choose what you say than say what you choose.

Anonymous

MENTALS

1. I am going to tell my mom! . . . Please do, I have wanted to meet her.
2. You gonna' count me tardy? . . . Certainly not! I am going to count you early for your next period.
3. It wasn't my fault! . . . Forget it, we'll have a random drawing to determine fault.
4. You can't make me to do this! . . . No, but I can make you disappear.
5. This is stupid! . . . Then you should be able to do it.
6. Why are you making me do this? . . . Because I am into power.
7. You are ruining the best years of my life . . . Yes, after puberty, it is downhill.
8. Can I sharpen my pencil? . . . I don't know, can you?
9. I don't have it . . . Thank you for considering my paper load.
10. YOU GAVE me an "F" . . . Sorry, I didn't know it was a gift.
11. I don't have a pencil . . . Neither does the bum on the street.
12. I am going to the principal! . . . If you get an appointment, let me know. I haven't seen him for days.
13. You are giving me an assigned seat? . . . Pack your peechee; I am into neighborhood renewal.
14. I wasn't talking! . . . That's right; I forgot you front as a ventriloquist's dummy.
15. Can I go to the bathroom? . . . Certainly not here!
16. I was absent yesterday . . . Mentally or physically?
17. How long should this be? . . . According to my calculations, about 16.3 centimeters.

18. Oh, God, this isn't fair! . . . Somehow, I think God has more important things to do than think about your quiz grade.
19. This is hard! . . . I forgot; you only get easy "stuff."
20. I am going to my counselor! . . . Me, too!

❦

Wise men say nothing in dangerous times.

John Selden

TEACHING TUG OF WARS

Sometimes, during a class discussion, a teacher's and student's viewpoints collide. Each on the other side, each hoping to force the other to give up his convictions and admit the error of his ways. Faces grow taut. Voices ring with control. Each contestant strains against the other's argument, grabbing any slack in thought to keep the opponent off balance. With a twist of words, the line of tension tightens. Digging in, weighing his tone, pulling back from tolerance, listening and reason, the victor senses the win. One final jerk and the struggle ends. The master teacher knows winners do not drag losers through the mud while staying clean themselves. Classroom tug of wars are better left on the outside where it is acceptable to play in the dirt.

❦

A word too much always defeats its purpose.

Arthur Schopenhauer

HIGH NOON

Within each of us resides the resident gunslinger. He bluffed his way into our presence by promising to protect us from disappointment and to keep us out of harm's way. We use him very little, but know he can be summoned at a moment's notice to give "our" best shot. He has a swagger and can draw upon conclusions faster than the unaware. If he's not kept under control, he's deadly and will shoot a new idea full of holes without even flinching. His aim is pointed at risk, innovation and creativity. Rapid-fire questions, smirks and ambushes are his partners. He rides into our classroom or meetings in the afternoon when he knows we are most tired and entertains himself by refusing to listen, sharing sarcasm or bullying with his demonstrations of target practice.

Many teachers control their hired gun and do not give him free rein without awareness. They believe sometimes his use in a "battle" is necessary but know he has no loyalties, and his price is often steep: anger, humiliation and the loss of collegial esteem. The best teachers dodge his bullets, watch for misfires and refuse his services. These professionals have learned a hired gun is not an answer but a parting shot that can backfire.

❦

You can't shoot an idea.

Thomas Dewey

FATIGUE

The length of the teaching day often begins at sunrise and ends as the sunlight slides into the evening shadows. Each moment has been spent with children's questions, administrative desires, curriculum materials, parents' concerns and collegues' needs. The long hours become cyclical; the sheer energy required to teach, care and interact is overwhelming, so much to do and yet the feeling of so little time.

Learn to stop working. Let the bone-weary fatigue sweep over you; heed its message. Though all may not be done on your checklist, remember that quality, not quantity, is teaching's partner. Shut the door to your classroom and its ties, and open a present for yourself. Let the teaching day end. Take a walk, savor a hot cup of tea, snuggle with someone you love, read a favorite book, listen to music or just sit and enjoy the silence, all a gift for you. It is okay to stop unfinished, for tomorrow is promised. You are much more than the sum total of your teaching experiences.

❦

Listen: there's a hell
of a good universe next door: let's go.

E. E. Cummings

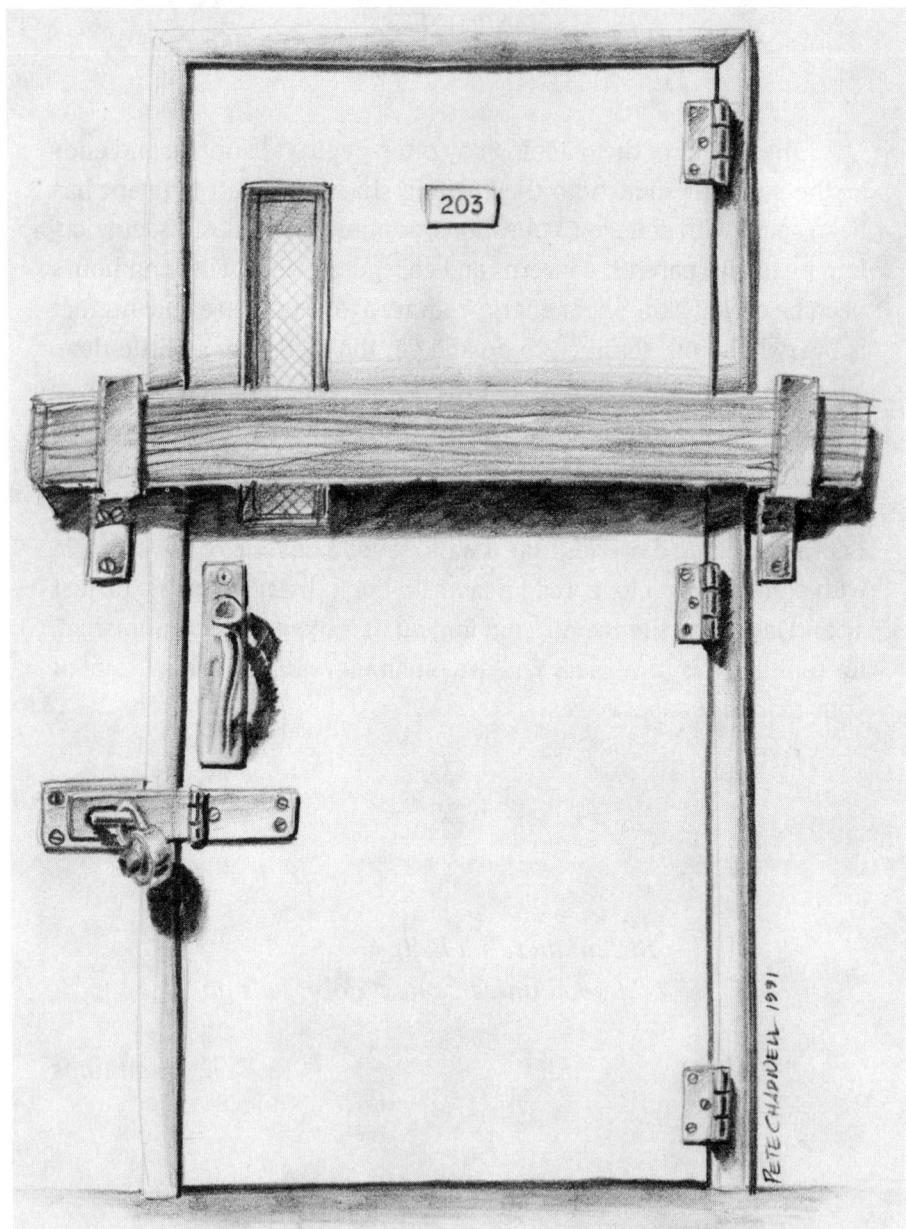

ISOLATION

Sometimes it just seems like too much energy is needed to be with or talk to colleagues. For most, this feeling is temporary, and we seek renewal in spaces of solitude. For others, isolation creeps into its place. A door is shut, a wall is built and school becomes a cold and lonely house.

Take the time to notice your peers. Make a special effort to say good morning to someone you don't often see, write a congratulations note to a colleague who's done something special, offer to help another teacher who's stressed. Share an idea or a joke with someone down the hall. Knock on a closed door in your school.

❦

Friendship needs no words — it is solitude delivered from the anguish of loneliness.

Dag Hammerskjold

DUALITIES

Teaching schedules are imposed, bells ring, interruptions seem endless . . . chaos within order. Evaluations occur, new programs are implanted and old ideas are abandoned . . . destruction within creativity. Education is proclaimed of national interest, programs are cut and budgets slashed . . . expectation within reality. The stress caused while trying to stay centered between the dualities can be extraordinary.

Solitude . . . . Collegiality
Objectivity . . . . Caring
Limited Time . . . . More requirements
Team Work . . . . Individuality
Order . . . . Creativity
Academics . . . . Activities
Active . . . . Passive
Job expectations . . . . . Individual needs

And so the list goes on . . . learn to reflect on the dualities of extremes. Grow to understand your balancing act.

❧

In formal logic, a contradiction is the signal of a defeat; but in the evolution of real knowledge it marks the first step in progress towards a victory.

Alfred North Whitehead

A MAZING

Gossip ... rumors ... talk whispered idly in the hallways, shared in the faculty lounge, embellished in the parking lot. Like a labyrinth tunnel each twist and turn promises to be going somewhere only to entangle the speakers in a false escape. With each repetition of the wind of words, the more intricate the puzzle, the less chance of a direct passage out. Some of our colleagues spend a lifetime in these catacombs creating new tunnels and false fronts; others flounder trying to weave their way through the maze while listening to the direction givers. When being lured into the pattern, beware of your tunnel vision and watch your step. The savvy, caring teacher knows going in is always much easier than coming out. And the energy expended on searching for an exit is energy better used for blocking the entrance.

❦

Truth is often eclipsed but never extinguished.

Livy

CHANGE ARTISTS

Education is a profession that requires the teacher to maintain balance in a sea of constant flux. And so it is that we become the master change artists. We know that ten pennies do not equal more power than a dime, but offer a different perspective. The evolutionist among us prefers to create change in a slow, directed progression by buying a piece of the action a penny a payment. However, the revolutionist, impatient by nature, will not buy into a time payment plan but spends one coin equal to the ten and creates the change in a single transaction. Though the price of the vision remains the same, the style of purchase varies. Evolutionist? Revolutionist? Spend your dime wisely.

❦

The art of progress is to preserve order amid change
and to preserve change amid order.

Alfred North Whitehead

PERSPECTIVE

Sometimes the needs or traumas in the teaching profession can be overwhelming. Some events matter so much, the hurts are so deep, and the joys so great all else seems less important than the moment at hand. And yet, *at that very second*, people on our planet are starving to death, many homeless are wishing for a night by a warm hearth, and a mother is giving birth to a new life.

Some archaeologists say that humankind has been on this earth only seconds in relation to the geological age of our planet. This knowledge places each joy or sorrow within a compendium of time. When involvement threatens to swallow you, remember to save some energy and caring for the battles and celebrations of tomorrow. Face each teaching moment with a kind heart laced with the remembrance of nature's grandeur and the joys of new life. A broader view of our planet and humankind will keep the hurts less harsh, the joys more treasured and the inner peace more constant. Perspective is your center.

❦

When a man is wrapped up in himself, he becomes
a pretty small package.

John Ruskin

THE A

```
                    ********
                 *   Success   *
                *  Professional  *
               *  React    Ignore  *
              *  Mentor    Learner  *
             *  Logic        Emotion  *
            *  Facts          Intuition  *
           *  Facilitate        Direct  *
          *  Quality          Quantity  *
         *  Caregiver   ****    Enabler  *
        *  Power        *   *  Empower  *
       *  Solitude     *    *  Loneliness  *
      *  Listening    *       *  Speaking  *
     *  Arbitrator   *        *   Leader  *
    *  Participant  ****************  Observer  *
   *  Flexibility .......Balance........ Rigidity  *
  *  Reflection    ********    Spontaneity  *
 *  Playfulness   *      *    Seriousness  *
*  Thoroughness  *        *  Incompletion  *
*  Traditional  *          *  Experimental  *
*  Competition *            *  Collaboration  *
*  Perspective *             *  Rationalization  *
*********************        *******************
```

It is style which complements affirmation with limitation and with humility; it is style which makes it possible to act effectively, but not absolutely; it is style which enables us to find harmony between the pursuit of ends essential to us, and the regard for views, the sensibilities, the aspirations of others; it is style which is the deference that action pays to uncertainty; it is above all style through which power defers to reason.

J. Robert Oppenheimer

❦

MISTAKES

As a teacher you know mistakes are correctable and, in most cases, the damage done can be mended. Sometimes a simple, "I was wrong, and you were right" will do the trick. Occasionally, the repair takes a little longer and requires more. Teachers accept mistakes from their pupils as part of the learning process; good teachers allow their colleagues and themselves the same right. When was the last time you openly admitted to a student, colleague or yourself that you were wrong? Once an error is accepted, the learning and growing can begin. Isn't that what teaching is all about?

❦

The man who makes no mistakes
does not usually make anything.

Bishop W. C. Magee

HOLD 'EM

Good teachers know active learning requires each student to take a risk and make an individual investment to get a piece of the action. Sometimes upping the ante too soon will cause some students to fold too early while others may sit quietly by willing to call if they believe the teacher is bluffing. Playing each hand carefully we generally split pairs only when the situation demands action. We learn to recognize and use the joker to compliment rather than disrupt the lesson. We play a straight whenever we can, are sometimes beaten by a full house and rarely use the royal flush. Often we hold an ace in the hole, play our hunches with tantalizing skill and share the winnings with each participant. We know the stakes are high and the losses can break the house. In teaching, winning is predicated upon the success of others, and we must play each hand we are dealt with the skill and finesse of the high stakes gambler.

❦

The game of life is not so much holding a
good hand as playing a poor hand well.

H. T. Leslie

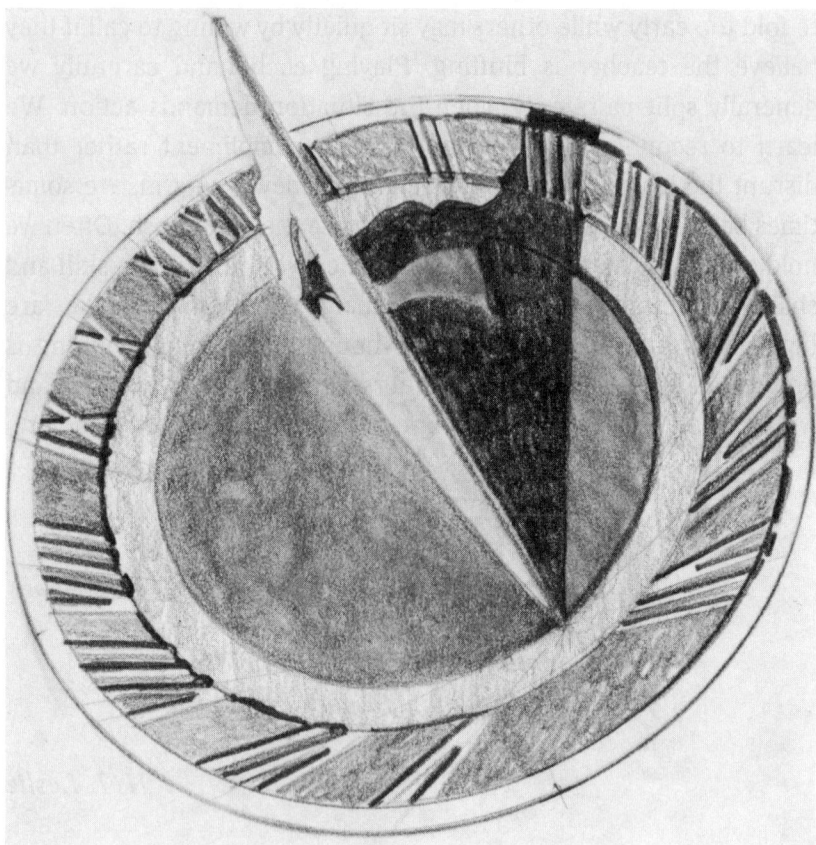

TIME

Moment by moment, hour by hour, day by day, you work as a trader in time. Yet, time is the great equalizer; the administrator in the office, the teacher and student in the classroom and the prisoner in the cell are all allotted only twenty-four hours in each day. No matter how much time is borrowed, bought or stolen, twenty-four hours is our common denominator . . . no more, no less. The passing of time refuses our interruptions; we cannot slow it or stop it. Time is our silent partner who never cries out in pain if it is wasted or joy if it is spent wisely. We coin terms like "wait time" and "time on task" to measure the sometimes immeasurables. As travelers dealing in time trades determining not only the quality of our journey but the journey of others, we know anger wastes time, learning saves time and caring takes time.

❦

The butterfly counts not months but moments,
and has time enough.

Rabindranath Tagore

STARS

An enormous amount of energy was expended designing THE LESSON. Thought-provoking questions were carefully selected, the activity painstakingly prepared and the introduction arranged to snare the most wily students practicing learning avoidance. All enthusiasm and energy were exhausted during the presentation. Alas, the extensive preparation captured only one student in the front row; the high-powered questions intrigued only yourself. Reception to the activity made you use the skills of a lion tamer.

In teaching, time invested can yield small return. Remember, many, many best-selling, critically acclaimed novels were rewritten and rejected a multitude of times before success was celebrated. So, if a well-planned lesson is ineffective and falls upon the deaf ears of the disinterested, know that you may be joining the ranks of the rich and famous.

❦

Only a mediocre is always at his best.

Somerset Maugham

BAROMETER

In the last years, many of our colleagues have left the teaching ranks; some have retired while others have just quit. Ours is a job that can create tremendous stress and feelings of futility. The media rarely praises teachers but wholeheartedly heralds news of studies that Johnny is unable to read, write, compute or think. The implication is that the teachers and the schools are doing a poorer job. Yet, teachers continue to work extraordinarily hard.

The average teacher has hundreds of interactions a day and performs a multitude of individual tasks per hour. Both the urban and rural teacher experience student verbal abuse. Many students spend more time in front of the television than participating in the classroom. The list goes on. It is no wonder that the voices of depression, stress, and frustration whisper within our ranks. Ours is an uphill climb. Our professional self-esteem must come from within. On those "tough" days, take the time for barometer check:

1. When was the last time you gave praise to a student for a job well done?
2. When did you last share a genuine laugh with a student?
3. When did you last give a student extra help?
4. When was the last time you served on a building or district committee?
5. How often do you help out with extracurricular activities beyond the school day?

6. Have you attended any inservices lately?
7. When was the last time you had a parent contact?
8. How often do you talk shop with a colleague?
9. How much mental energy did you expend on teaching activities last weekend?
10. When did you last help a colleague?

You *have* been busy: caring, teaching and giving.
You are a professional.

❦

Teaching is not a lost art, but the regard
for it is a lost tradition.

Jaques Barzun

SCHIZOID

Successful teachers have perfected the art of practiced schizophrenia. A master teacher will find nothing unusual in sternly disciplining one student by facial expression, tone or tongue only to turn seconds later to warmly praise or encourage another student. Acting the schizoid becomes not only natural for the veteran teacher, but necessary. Though Corbett Thigpen may have written *The Three Faces of Eve*, veteran teachers live it daily.

❦

Schizophrenia (divided mind — or split soul)

Paul E. Bleuler

INSIGHTS

I am a(n) _____ professional who is known by my colleagues for my _____, and _____. If my students were to describe me, the three words which would come up the most often would be _____, _____, and _____. Though I think my greatest weakness as a teacher is my inability to be more _____, this "gap" is balanced by my strength to be _____. Since I have improved much in the area of _____, this year I will focus on _____. As a staff member, I have the most difficulty working with colleagues who lack the ability to be _____. On the other hand, I most admire those peers who demonstrate _____ and _____. Though I wish this staff were more _____, I think we are especially skilled in _____.

In the classroom I am most drawn to those students who have the quality of _____ and most frustrated by those who exhibit poor _____. I wish my students as a whole were more _____. To help them practice this I will be more _____. Because survival, personal satisfaction and success may be hard for some students to achieve in their future, I would hope that they learn _____, _____, and _____ are enormously helpful qualities.

❦

A moment's insight is sometimes worth a life's experience.

Oliver Wendell Holmes

WORD LIST (FILL IN)
FOR INSIGHTS

CAREGIVER, CARING, CARE
CHALLENGER, CHALLENGING, CHALLENGE
COLLABORATOR, COLLABORATION, COLLABORATE
COMPETITOR, COMPETITIVE, COMPETE
CONFIDENT, CONFIDENCE
CONSISTENT, CONSISTENCY
COOPERATION, COOPERATE, COOPERATIVE
CURIOSITY, CURIOUS
CREATIVITY, CREATIVE, CREATE
DIGNITY, DIGNIFIED
DISCIPLINARIAN, DISCIPLINE
ENERGY, ENERGETIC
ENTHUSIASM, ENTHUSIASTIC
EXPERIMENT, EXPERMENTATIVE, EXPERIMENTAL
FACILITATOR, FACILITATE, FACILITATING
FLEXIBILITY, FLEXIBLE
HUMOR, HUMOROUS
INDEPENDENCE, INDEPENDENT
INTEGRITY
INTUITION, INTUITIVE
INVOLVEMENT, INVOLVED, INVOLVE
KNOWLEDGEABLE
LISTENER, LISTENING, LISTENING SKILLS
MOTIVATION, MOTIVATED, MOTIVATION, MOTIVATE
ORGANIZATION, ORGANIZE, ORGANIZED
PATIENCE, PATIENT
PERSISTENCE, PERSISTENT, PERSIST

REFLECTIVE, REFLECT, REFLECTION
RESPONSIBILITY, RESPONSIBLE
SPEAKER, SPEAKING SKILLS, SPEAKS UP
SATISFACTION, SATISFIED
SERIOUSNESS, SERIOUS
THOROUGH, THOROUGHNESS
TOLERATION, TOLERATE, TOLERANT
VISION, VISIONARY

❧

AWOL
(ABSENT WITHOUT LESSON)

You tossed and turned all night long; you are running a fever, and every bone in your body aches. Your one wish is that you could call in sick and then spend the day "in comfort." Alas, being sick for a teacher is not that simple; unlike most jobs, you are accountable for what goes on in your classroom whether you are there or not. The assumption is, of course, that a substitute will be able to follow your weekly plan, but in many cases, we know this is not possible because the substitute may not be skilled in your area, may not have the knowledge background necessary to continue with your lesson or may not have the discipline skills to create a learning environment. Knowing this, several options run through your pounding head:

1. Call in and tell "them" that you are too ill to plan a lesson for the substitute but that since all the administrators are educators, you are counting on them to come up with something.
2. Try to get a movie to show. (Know any video stores that deliver at 8 a.m.?)
3. Give the classes a study hall hoping the substitute will understand.
4. Drag yourself out of bed and write a detailed, valid lesson plan the substitute can handle which includes all the administrivia she will need to know to function adequately. (Also, you must figure out how to deliver the lesson plan to your building, a minor inconvenience for someone who is dying.)

5. Forget that you have the flu, feel like death warmed over, and are planning your funeral and go in to school anyway...it's almost easier.

The decision rests solely with you. You may select the last choice because the energy required to *not be there* is sometimes more demanding than the energy to be there. So what if you function like a zombie, resemble a corpse and feel that you have only a few hours of life left? Like the mailman, you deliver no matter the weather. Being sick and being a teacher isn't easy.

❦

Doctors think a lot of patients are cured
who have simply given up in disgust.

Don Herold

TEACHERS

To teach is to learn.

Japanese Proverb

*A teacher who is attempting to teach without inspiring
the pupil with a desire to learn is hammering on cold iron.*

Horace Mann

The art of teaching is the art of assisting discovery.

Mark Van Doren

*I beg of you to stop apologizing for being a member
of the most important . . . profession in the world.*

William G. Carr

*The teacher, like the artist, the philosopher, and the man of letters,
can perform his work adequately only if he feels himself to be an
individual directed by an inner creative impulse, not dominated
and fettered by outside authority.*

Bertrand Russell

In teaching it is the method and not the content that is the message . . . the drawing out, not the pumping in.

Ashley Montagu

Today the teacher no longer carries all knowledge within his brain. He does not transmit knowledge so much as feed it to each individual. He steps in to excite curiosity, to guide pupils toward knowledge, and to see that they have acquired it. It is up to the pupil to assume his responsibilities, to conquer knowledge independently with the reward of self-realization. Teaching is selflessness in service of others.

Berlie J. Fallon

❦

JOB PERFECT

Imagine . . . your alarm goes off, you spring out of bed with a smile because you know that you are about to experience the PERFECT TEACHING DAY! What will it be like?

1. When you arrive at school, a parking place just where you want to park is open.

2. You walk into the building and everyone offers a friendly "Good morning" or "How's it going?"

3. You check your mail and find nothing insulting, anxiety-creating or needlessly time-taking. However, there is a note from the principal thanking you for a "job well done."

4. When you get to your classroom, you discover that the thermostat works, and you will be able to teach in the optimum climate, not too hot, not too cold.

5. The janitor has done a superb job. The floor has been swept, the trash emptied, the board cleaned and a general feeling of well-being permeates the room.

6. The bell rings and all your students come into your classroom smiling, well fed, lovingly groomed, and ready to learn.

7. The morning announcements are read and are concise, clear, positive and accurate.

8. When you begin your lessons, all the necessary materials are available. You have a book for every student, and the worksheets are printed clearly enough that you do not have to translate the words from "ditto slur" to "English clear." The projector or overhead is working.

9. During your lesson there are no interruptions; you are able to teach without the intercom coming on, messages being delivered, fire drills intruding or students coming and going.

10. Everyone has his/her homework completed, and you do not have to listen to excuses, rationalizations or fabrications.

11. Not one of your students whines, complains or is rude.

12. The lessons you so carefully planned work well; within your room, everyone is attentive, interested and actively involved. Learning is the outcome.

13. You have a planning period that is duty-free AND not interrupted. You are able to efficiently correct a set of papers, check and adjust your lesson plans for the next day and have a moment just to think.

14. Though for lunch you eat cafeteria food, you find the meal a gourmet's delight. Your lunch hour is leisurely and restful.

15. After lunch while on your way to class, you are stopped by a student who is still excited by your morning lesson.

16. Later in the afternoon, you check your mail and find a note from a parent thanking you for your effort with her child and another note from a peer which brings a smile to your face.

17. After the last bell rings, you look around and find that for that day nothing is leaking, broken, missing or lost.

18. You finish up your day by correcting some papers, entering grades and tying up the loose ends. The feeling of satisfaction slips over you like a comfortable sweater; you gather yourself together and walk into a beautiful afternoon.

Though you may never have had a day like this, what would make a perfect teaching day for you?

❦

In small proportions we just beauties see,
And in short measures life may perfect be.

Ben Johnson

PERSEVERANCE

Perseverance loves challenges. Lithe, lean and incredibly athletic she can climb over the most difficult barriers, swim in the swiftest of currents and wait the longest time. Some people say she is not a good listener because she doesn't seem to hear the words "no, impossible, quit or can't." She is rarely rushed. Laughingly she explains time is given to her whether she uses it or not. She is the best of friends because she will not abandon you. She has been heard to quietly explain that it is not a surprise to her that "giving up" contains eight letters and "getting up" contains nine. She says "Of course, standing takes more energy than lying down." She visits the young, but generally lives more comfortably with those older. She stays only when her two sisters, Persistence and Patience, feel at home.

The best teachers understand she offers strength to the weak, an edge for the slow and endurance for the determined. Because she is shy and takes a long time to get to know, they introduce her to students slowly, coax her with tidbits of praise and acceptance and allow her to train like any Olympic athlete.

❦

Triumph is just the "umph" behind "try."

Anonymous

SETTLEMENTS

If you have taught long enough, you have probably observed a situation where a peer's abilities and skills have come under administrative "attack." Sometimes this person's incompetency has been a source of amusement in faculty lounge discussions. "Gees, did you hear what happened to Smith? You didn't! He got caught showing another of his film extravaganzas, *Africa Today, 1957*, during the Australia unit. It's hard to believe that the administration puts up with him, but somebody has to set our standards!" Or brought to your attention by students' off-handed remarks, "It's okay if I'm late to Smith's room; he doesn't care. All we ever do is watch stupid films. I won't miss anything!" Or jokingly referred to in Friday night get-togethers, "The movie *Rocky* and all its sequels have already been booked by Smith for right after spring break . . . Oughta' take several weeks. He's doing a unit on the underachiever returns!" Or discussed within the privacy of a home, "I would never want my child to take a class from Smith. He's an embarrassment to the profession."

Then, strangely, some of the colleagues who have openly criticized his teaching, circle the wagons around the "victim," and begin to publicly defend him to others while taking warning shots at the attackers. The building climate turns cold and untrusting; trenches dug and "us against them" prevails. "United we stand; divided we fall" echoes up and down the line. And though we helped inflict some of the victim's wounds, some of our peers turn on the attackers with a vengeance. Someone in the rank and file says quietly, "I agree with the administrative position, but I think they should have been kinder." A few nods of assent and the huddle pulls closer together. "What will he do for his retirement? What about his dignity and feeling of self-worth? He's dedicated his life to education!

Shouldn't 'they' be held responsible, after all, 'they' hired him?"

The issue becomes crowded with feelings, facts and fears; what was once common knowledge is now whispered with uncertainty. Those who had once judged Smith's skills and found them wanting, now sit in judgement of the other side. Loyalties shift.

Just as we know that being a parent does not guarantee being a good mother or father, being a teacher does not guarantee good teaching. In both cases child support is often the issue but is lost in the accusations and fury of the threatened separation . . . a divorce gone public.

❦

Let us not look back in anger or forward in fear,
but around in awareness.

James Thurber

PETE CHADWELL

78   TEACHING REFLECTIONS

HEALING

A tidal wave towering above the shoreline smashes the landscape with unrestrained power. Left? A broken, debris-strewn waterfront. Though much of the ruins are pulled to the sea by the receding action, and eventually, the beach is swept clean again, scars left by the thunderous force still remain for the perceptive observer. It takes time for nature to heal wounds just as it does for the teacher to help a scarred child. If you feel the frustration of little success with one of life's wounded, remember, you are the calm, consistent sea of love that will wash over the child time and time again. There is no calendar for the healing, only your caring.

❦

We are children of our landscape.

Lawrence Durrell

FILM FINALES

Finally, after cajoling, threatening, haggling and looking around the building yourself, you have located a projector to show the film you ordered weeks ago and planned to show yesterday. However, yesterday the projector you were promised failed to arrive . . . but that's another story. You've prepped your students, given them a moment to arrange their seats so all can see and then you turn off the lights. Darkness invades the room. Giggles emanate from the back corner, then silence. You turn on the projector, the light flashes onto the screen then begins to flicker as the images bounce and the sound track chatters. The lights are turned back on and the film rethreaded while your students sit quietly talking among themselves. The lights go out; the film starts again. Although a bit out of focus, everything else seems to be okay. You relax. Then unexpectedly the room goes entirely black, there are no images on the screen, but you can hear the projector running. Groans interrupt the darkness. the lights go on; the bulb has burned out. You send a student to the a-v room to get a replacement. (Your students are noticebly more restless. You apologize for the inconvenience which they accept with good humor.) After what seems like an inordinate amount of time, the student returns with a bulb and tells you he had to "run all over" before he could find help. Quickly you exchange bulbs, settle the students, turn out the lights and adjust the focus and sound. The images flash upon the screen again; at last, everything seems to be working. Moments later the bell rings; some of the students jump up and stumble out in the dark while others sit in their seats and yell at their peers to turn on the lights. The period is over; the film is half done (though it must be returned by 4 o'clock), and you are exhausted. You stand up, press the rewind button, shut your classroom door and wonder what the ITIP people would say about that lesson closure.

❦

If anything can go wrong, it will.

Murphy's Law

IF . . .

1. If you were asked to select two critical teacher qualities, what would they be?

2. If given an opportunity to thank a colleague for a job well done, who would it be and why?

3. If you shared with your faculty one thing you excel in, which skill or quality would you choose?

4. If you were given the power, what one aspect of the teaching profession would you change and why?

5. If asked, what would you say has been your biggest challenge in teaching?

6. If you had to suggest three books for a faculty reading list, what would you select?

7. If you visited your teaching future five years from now, what would you see?

8. If given the opportunity and needed support, which of your teaching skills would you most like to change?

9. If you were given a public forum, what three ideas about education would you most like to share?

10. If given the task to design a school-wide grading policy, what elements would you include and why?

11. If you were told to share one piece of personal information about yourself with your students, what would you share?

12. If you were given the opportunity to conduct educational research, what would you focus on and why?

13. If you were a principal, what would be your number-one priority and how would you accomplish it?

14. If you could contact one of your own teachers, who would you contact and what would you say?

15. If limited to posting only three classroom rules, what would they be and why?

16. If given the opportunity to share your favorite teaching "war" story, which one would it be?

17. If you were writing a book for new teachers, what are the three most important things you would tell them?

18. If given an opportunity to eavesdrop on a student conversation about yourself, what would you hear?

19. If given the power to instill one quality within your students, which quality would you select?

20. If given the opportunity what, if anything, would you change about your career path?

21. If you could relive one teaching experience, which would it be?

22. If you could pick the type of students you would have in your classroom, what four adjectives would describe them?

23. If you had to share your most humorous teaching experience, what would it be?

24. If you could select the next building principal, what three qualities would you look for?

25. If told that you were in charge of the building budget, what would your priorities be?

I keep six honest serving men.
They taught me all I knew:
Their names are What and Why and When
And How and Where and Who.

Rudyard Kipling

TEACHING REFLECTIONS 🌑 83

THE CLIMB

The peaks and valleys of teaching offer a unique challenge. Many attempts to reach the heights will be met with success, though others will be shaded with disappointment. The successes will etch themselves in your memory while the disappointments will become the learning times. Plan carefully, but, if the trek is unsuccessful, do not stay in the mountain's shadow, for it is cold there. Learn to heal your wounds, for like the climber, a new season will often bring a second chance.

❦

He that can't endure the bad will
not live to see the good.

Anonymous

BEYOND THE CALL

The question is, can you juggle a book, an apple, two erasers, and a piece of chalk at one time without letting any single item hit the ground? If you can, you have chosen the correct profession. Once you get your classroom organized, there will be a committee for you to serve on; once the committee gets off the ground, there will be a club for you to advise. Once your club is under control, you will be given a new class to teach or another duty to perform. Sleight-of-hand and agility settle in as friends; a master juggler is born.

❦

Thrusting my nose firmly between his teeth, I threw him heavily to the ground on top of me.

Mark Twain

PASSAGES

After years of teaching the same age level or content field, boredom may be replacing the first years of enthusiasm. A future progression of years teaching the same subject matter does not excite you any more. Creativity within your lesson design may not be the motivating, energizing factor it once was. You discover you are effective within your classroom but must no longer spend the endless weekend hours creating that effectiveness. The thought of taking more classes may be an irritant rather than a stimulant. Your retirement investment not only offers your future, but can sometimes feel like a prison. You do not want to jeopardize its promise, so with resignation, you dutifully return to your educational cell. However, through all this inner turmoil, you remain the dedicated teacher. You don't show your frustration; you work hard, you care, and you are effective.

1. What if you quietly started getting another degree or education? . . . The time will pass with or without your energies.

2. What if you designed a new course and implemented it? . . . Energy comes from innovation.

3. What if you decided to renew an interest in a hobby you have put aside? . . . Satisfaction is the by-product of involvement.

4. What if you learned to do something entirely new? . . . Renewal comes from fresh challenges.

5. What if you do nothing differently? . . . Frustration and boredom have been purchased.

I want to talk about another high country now in the world of thought . . . the high country of the mind . . . Few people travel here . . . In the high country of the mind, one has to become adjusted to the thin air of uncertainty.

Robert Prisig
Zen and the Art of
Motorcycle Maintenance

❦

"ALL THE WORLD'S A STAGE . . . "

A teaching colleague once said, "I do six shows a day and hassle all hecklers." Though teaching is a reality based profession interlaced with the drama of real life, sometimes our days reflect *Miami Vice, Jeopardy* or the *Wheel of Fortune*. Indeed, we are often the script writer, director, producer and the actor or actress who can give an academy award performance upon demand. Our show must go on through sickness, health, peace or pandemonium. Think about your finest performance. Treasure your Oscar; you earned it.

❦

Never meddle with play actors, for they're a favored race.

Cervantes

THE LONG STRETCH

Can you meet with Mr. and Mrs. Smith at 2:50 today? Can you help me after school? Is it okay if I turn my paper in late? I have a good reason. Will you be able to attend the curriculum meeting after school? Don't forget to turn in the report on Tiff Baclar before you go home. Can you pick up the film projector yourself? All our aides are busy. Don't forget the grade level meeting during lunch. Please call Mr. Fantion before 3:30. Could you locate that article on parent conferencing today? I would really like to read it tonight. Can you take my place on hall duty this afternoon during your prep period? And so it goes . . . the peppering and punctuating of requests and questions.

By day's end you are exhausted. A student asks for your help by saying, "This is hard. I don't understand." With stinging sarcasm you answer with, "Of course you don't understand, neither does the bum sleeping on the park bench. Learn to stay awake!" The student slinks back to his desk, shuts his book and quits trying.

Remember, you can only stretch a rubber band so far. To keep from snapping, learn to quietly say no to some of the demands which pull you on "bad" days.

❧

Words are one of our chief means of adjusting to all the situations of life. The better control we have over our words, the more successful our adjustment is likely to be.

Bergen Evans

TEACHER TERMINOLOGY

Peer coaching . . . peeking at a colleague's game plan
Wait time . . . counting the days before a much-needed vacation
Time on task . . . years of teaching
Tracking . . . what students do on a rainy day
Faculties . . . what you may lose before the year's end
Planning periods . . . the day's punctuation
Fire drill . . . announcement of pay day
Pep assemblies . . . Friday afternoon get-togethers
Rally squad . . . colleagues who support you
Students at risk . . . those who talk back to you
Set . . . order given to students
Closure . . . short in "teacher talk" for close your book, close your
    mouth, close the door
Lesson plan . . . what you would follow if you had the time
Committees . . . those who have been committed
Veterans . . . colleagues who have "extra" staples, chalk and tape
Termination . . . end of the semester
Classroom . . . room with excellent bulletin boards
Overhead . . . missile that misses you
Homework . . . windows, laundry, dinner
Team teaching . . . class loaded with "jocks"
Faculty meetings . . . checking for all your senses
Student objectives . . . reasons given for not doing assignments
Detention . . . the stress factor

❦

CHOICES

Two veteran teachers walking down the hall see a third teacher struggling with a load of books. Both glance at one another knowingly and shake their heads. One whispers poor old Smith is such a crabby, morose teacher he deserves to struggle with the texts just as everyone has to struggle with him. The other colleague, though nodding in agreement, steps forward and takes some of the books from Smith's stack saying, "Here, let me help. You lead the way." Frowning Mr. Smith grumbles that he doesn't need any help; but, turning on his heels, he leads the way towards his classroom.

Later that day at lunch the two friends sit down together though one is noticeably miffed. Sighing, she frowns saying, "You know, I can't believe you. With all you know about Smith and what a jerk he is, you took your time to help him. I bet he's never helped you. I can't believe you carried all those books for him; he obviously did not want your help!"

The friend smiles slowly answering, "And I can't believe that you are still carrying those books; I put my stack down hours ago." (Adaptation from Zen Buddhist story)

❧

Our dignity is not in what we do
but what we understand.

George Santayana

GARDENS

During the spring the seeds of knowledge sown earlier begin to sprout. Surprises abound. Some of the new growth offers tall, straight, luxuriant limbs that seemingly shot up overnight and, now, constantly wave in their rows almost edging out those of lesser energy and slower growth. We begin to cull, ridding our space of some of the tenacious pests who have become general nuisances and threaten the health of the entire patch. Some of the young sprouts are not in the neat tidy rows we carefully plotted but have obstinately established themselves in between. We uproot and transplant a few of these independents while others are unavoidably stepped on or left to flourish unattended. We toil daily in our field of young promise carefully cultivating each new bud.

Finallly, after nine months of watchful nurturing, the fruits of our hard labors are harvested. But, as with all master gardeners, no sooner than the clean-up ends do we begin planning for next year's crop.

❦

But though I am an old man,
I am but a young gardener.

Thomas Jefferson

THE CHILD WITHIN

I haven't been on this earth very long and there is so much to learn. Mom said that's why I have to go to school. Lots of the time I am afraid of something, and sometimes I want to hide. Things happen so fast. When I talk, sometimes I think that nobody listens but me, and I already know what I said. Once in awhile I don't do what I'm told 'cuz it doesn't make sense to me. And sometimes I just don't do it because I don't feel like it; besides, I want to do the tellin' once in awhile. I like attention; it makes me feel important. Most of the time I try pretty hard to do what's right, but when I get mad, I can be pretty bad. Sometimes I wish everyone would just go away and let me alone. I like to have friends, though. They make me feel good, and they care about what happens to me when other people don't. Sometimes, my friends can get me to laugh when nobody else can.

My mom says there is nobody like me in the whole world! And you know what? I haven't met anyone just like me, either. I think she's right; I am special! I wonder if my teacher will notice?

❧

At bottom every man knows well enough that
he is a unique being, only once on this
earth; and by no extraordinary chance will such a
marvelously picturesque piece of diversity in unity as
he is, ever be put together a second time.

Friedrich Nietzsche

GOOD THINGS

What's good about teaching? The laughter that sometimes accompanies the joys of learning . . . eyes dancing with pride after accomplishing a difficult new task . . . a colleague excitedly sharing craft knowledge . . . an ex-student thanking you for hours spent . . . a parent praising your efforts . . . that day when a student who has been "wounded" in one of life's battles begins to heal . . . a shy smile flashing a silent hello . . . a student's enthusiasm about what you're teaching . . . the incredible moment when your students soar on the wings of learning! What's good about teaching? Many, many things!

❦

*A teacher affects eternity; no one can tell
where his influence stops.*

Henry Adams

❧ TEACHING REFLECTIONS

SOLITUDE

The quiet stillness of peace that many of us seek after the day's intense demands is accomplished by listening to your inner source and sorting through the spent energies. Solitude gives space for reflection and restoration. Give yourself a personal moment by sharing some time with your best friend . . . you. Close your door, luxuriate in a long, slow stretch. Don't work; it will wait. You have spent the day on others. This space is yours.

❧

I never found a companion that was so companionable as solitude.

Henry David Thoreau

ABOUT THE AUTHOR

Raised in a small northern California town nestled snugly in the shadow of its namesake, Mt. Shasta, I grew up surrounded by mountains, lakes, and wilderness areas. With a loving family (including an older brother who was a favorite sidekick though I was careful not to tell him so), I spent endless hours and weekends exploring the nooks and crannies nature offered. Fishing, backpacking, horseback riding, belonging to the local 4-H and throwing myself into a myriad of school activities kept everyone constantly occupied. My love and appreciation of the wilderness was guided by my father. My quiet moments were spent reading and sharing my thoughts with a mother who encouraged visits to the library and local bookstores over the trancelike state fostered by hours of television viewing.

Upon high school graduation, I headed off to the University of Montana, miles from home, friends and family. I loved the independence of college, the challenge of the classes and, of course, the opportunity to meet so many people. However, when it came time to select an occupation, I was adrift. I can honestly say I went into teaching for all the wrong reasons, but I believe I stayed in teaching for all the right reasons. 1968 found me as a college graduate holding a BA in English and Library Science with a teaching certificate to boot, a husband and a teaching job in Sumner, Washington.

The teaching years which followed were intense, frustrating, energizing and overwhelming. I continued to take classes and freelance write. I explored gifted education, integrated curriculums, taught social studies, reading, English, worked as a school librarian, served as a department head, team coordinator and became heavily committed to the process we call education.

In the seventies, professional organizations caught my attention and I, along with thousands of teachers, struggled for collective bargaining and more control over our destinies in the classroom. Our battle cry stemmed from a growing sense of professionalism, frustration and desperation. During this time of political upheaval within the educational arena, I served in various union capacities ending my energy flow as the local association president.

In 1983, my personal life took a shift, and I found myself moving to Medford, Oregon, joining their school system as an English and social studies teacher and serving as department head for the humanities program. My pace slowed, and I had the luxury of reflecting on my 22-year-teaching journey. Over that time period, touched by thousands of students and parents and hundreds of teaching colleagues, I had developed a tremendous pride in what I did for a living and felt a great sense of respect and compassion for the everyday classroom teacher. The roots of the book, *Teaching Reflections,* began to take hold.

Also, during this time three colleagues and I formed an educational consulting company and, among other things, wrote the materials for the Senior Project Program which has won national and state awards. The success of the Senior Project Program has allowed me to visit with teachers and parents all over the nation reaffirming my beliefs and commitment to teaching.

Currently, I spend my time teaching, presenting seminars, writing, and enjoying life's journey with my companion and soulmate, my husband, John. *Teaching Reflections* is a singular expression of recognition to those often unheralded classroom heroes who spend their days teaching, interacting and giving to our nation's promise, our children.

For additional copies of *TEACHING REFLECTIONS*, telephone TOLL FREE 1-800-356-9315. MasterCard/VISA accepted.

To order *TEACHING REFLECTIONS* directly from the publisher, send your check or money order for $12.95 plus $2.75 shipping and handling ($15.70 postpaid) to: Rainbow Books, Inc., Order Dept., 1-T, P. O. Box 430, Highland City, FL 33846-0430.

For QUANTITY PURCHASES, telephone Rainbow Books, Inc., (813) 648-4420 or write to Rainbow Books, Inc., P. O. Box 430, Highland City, FL 33846-0430.